GW01159288

Original title:

The Smile Inside

Copyright © 2024 Creative Arts Management OÜ

All rights reserved.

Author: Clara Whitfield

ISBN HARDBACK: 978-9916-88-840-7

ISBN PAPERBACK: 978-9916-88-841-4

Radiant Spirits Unveiled

In the dawn's embrace we rise,
With whispers soft like lullabies.
Hearts ignited with pure delight,
Our souls ablaze, a wondrous light.

Through the fields of dreams we roam,
Finding strength in every home.
With every step, the truth we seek,
In laughter's grace, we find the peak.

Together we will stand and sing,
Celebrating what joy can bring.
With open arms and hearts so free,
We unveil the spirits meant to be.

In radiant hues, our stories blend,
A tapestry that will not end.
As sunlight dances on the day,
Our spirits shine in bright array.

The Light Beneath the Mask

Behind the smiles, a story lies,
In shadows deep, where secrets rise.
The mask we wear, a crafted guise,
Yet in our hearts, the truth defies.

Beneath the charm, a flicker glows,
A light that only the brave knows.
In silent nights, the fears we shed,
Awakening dreams that must be fed.

Though burdens weigh, we stand so tall,
Finding courage when we fall.
With laughter bright, we break the chains,
Revealing love where hope remains.

When daylight breaks, the masks will fade,
As every heartache finds its aid.
In radiant truth, we shall connect,
The light within we must protect.

Unspoken Joys of the Heart

In quiet moments, joy is born,
A simple glance, a rose with thorn.
The unvoiced dreams, the tender sighs,
In silence sweet, our spirits rise.

With every heartbeat, love unfolds,
A tapestry of warmth that holds.
In fleeting glances, worlds collide,
The sweetest truths we cannot hide.

Through gentle laughter, whispers play,
Creating bonds that guide our way.
In the depths of our shared embrace,
Unspoken joys find their rightful place.

Through midnight talks and morning light,
The heart reveals its softest sight.
In honest moments, truth gives birth,
To joy unspoken, full of worth.

Shadows of Laughter

In the twilight, shadows dance,
Laughter echoes, a fleeting chance.
With every chuckle, worries fade,
In joy's embrace, our fears are laid.

Beneath the moon, stories weave,
In playful jests, we dare believe.
With every giggle, bonds grow tight,
In shadows deep, we find the light.

Life's canvas painted in delight,
With strokes of color, we take flight.
Through trials shared and dreams pursued,
In laughter's realm, we are renewed.

So let us laugh, let voices soar,
In every joy, we find much more.
Together in these moments bright,
We light the world with pure delight.

Radiant Secrets

In the garden of whispers, truths bloom bright,
Hidden souls dance under the moonlight.
Each petal reveals what lies within,
Guarded dreams, secret joys begin.

Silent whispers exchanged in the air,
Light that travels through midnight's stare.
Unlocking the past with a gentle sigh,
Radiant secrets that never die.

Vivid Heartstrings

Strumming softly on strings of the heart,
Colors burst forth as the melodies start.
A canvas of sound, emotions intertwine,
Creating a symphony, pure and divine.

Each note a story, a memory spun,
Life's vivid threads woven into one.
In this bright dance of harmony's grace,
Every heart beats at its own pace.

Unseen Uplift

Beneath the surface, strength does reside,
A quiet power, no need to hide.
Wings of resilience, unseen yet strong,
Carrying dreams where they belong.

Subtle gestures of kindness shared,
Lifting spirits when no one dared.
In shadows they flourish, unbound and free,
Whispers of uplift, a soft symphony.

Undercover Joy

Smiles disguised in ordinary guise,
Hidden laughter behind weary eyes.
A spark in the mundane, a flicker of light,
Undercover joy, dancing out of sight.

In crowded places where silence prevails,
Jokes shared softly, unveiling tales.
A treasure tucked deep, yet bold in its flight,
Undercover joy, twinkling so bright.

Luminescence Restored

In shadows deep, we seek the light,
A flicker calls, dispells the night.
With every step, the hope will grow,
A radiant glow, in heart's warm flow.

The stars align, their beams converge,
Within our souls, the warmth will surge.
The past once dim, now brightly beams,
Embracing us with shining dreams.

Whimsical Whispers

In softest tones, the breezes sigh,
Through leafy trees where secrets lie.
A playful dance, the shadows weave,
As if the world will never grieve.

Bright petals laugh, in colors rare,
The spirits twirl, in joyful air.
With every glance, a wonder strikes,
In whispered jokes from nature's likes.

The Cheerful Core

At morning's light, we start anew,
With hearts aglow, the skies are blue.
Each smile shared, a gift to give,
A simple truth, a will to live.

In laughter's ring, our spirits soar,
A unity that's hard to ignore.
Together bound, we paint the day,
With joyous strokes, in love's ballet.

Unveiling Euphoria

Beyond the hills where sunlight streams,
Awaits the bliss, the silent dreams.
With arms wide open, we embrace,
The warmth of life, the sweet grace.

Each moment savored, rich and bright,
A tapestry of pure delight.
In every laughter, every sigh,
Unveiling joy, as time slips by.

Lively Subtleties

In shadows flicker soft delights,
A whispering breeze, a song takes flight.
Colors dance in subtle gleams,
Life's hidden truths, like vivid dreams.

The rustle of leaves, a fleeting touch,
Moments like these, we treasure so much.
Nature's sighs in gentle embrace,
Each day unfurls with quiet grace.

Ephemeral Gleams

Morning dew on petals bright,
Glimmers softly in the light.
Time slips by—oh, what a show,
Ephemeral, yet we long to know.

Sunset hues paint the evening sky,
Brushstrokes of gold as day waves goodbye.
Fleeting moments, captured in heart,
In memory's canvas, never to part.

The Light Found Within

In silence, we search for hidden sparks,
A glow that ignites in the deepest dark.
With every breath, the spirit sings,
Revealing the light that each life brings.

Walls may rise, the world may shake,
But within our souls, a fire wakes.
Embrace the warmth, let it unfold,
A story of courage, forever told.

Unveiling the Joy

Through laughter shared, the heart ignites,
In simple moments, pure delights.
Kindness blooms like flowers bright,
Unveiling joy, a wondrous sight.

Reach out your hand, let love unfold,
In every tale, new truths are told.
Together we dance, through highs and lows,
In union, the sweetest joy flows.

The Happy Veil

Beneath the sky, so bright and clear,
A joyful heart, we hold so dear.
In laughter's echo, spirits rise,
With every moment, love resides.

The colors dance in gentle sway,
While dreams of hope light up the day.
A warm embrace, a friendly smile,
Together we can share a while.

Through fields of joy, we skip and run,
With every step, our souls are spun.
The happy veil, a tapestry,
Of life and love, our symphony.

In whispered winds, our secrets told,
In stories shared, our hearts unfold.
With every dawn, a chance to thrive,
The happy veil keeps dreams alive.

Uplifted Spirits

When shadows fall and doubts arise,
We lift our hearts to brighter skies.
In every sigh, a chance to heal,
With every prayer, a strength we feel.

The morning sun brings light anew,
In every ray, a dream breaks through.
Together we can rising find,
With hopeful hearts, we leave behind.

Through troubled paths and winding ways,
We stand as one through all our days.
With uplifted spirits, we will soar,
Embracing love, forevermore.

With laughter's joy, we'll greet the morn,
In every heart, new dreams are born.
With every step, we walk in grace,
Uplifted spirits, time can't erase.

Beneath the Surface of Calm

In the stillness of the night,
Whispers blend with the stars' light,
Ripples dance on the lake's face,
Secrets held in nature's embrace.

Moonlight paints shadows that sigh,
Dreams afloat as the winds cry,
Peace wraps tight like a warm shawl,
Here, we flourish, and never fall.

Essence of Hidden Happiness

In quiet corners of the heart,
Laughter waits, a tender art,
Sunflowers gaze in the sun's shrine,
Each petal sings a joy divine.

Through the laughter and the tears,
Moments whisper through the years,
Find the light in shadows cast,
Essence of dreams that hold us fast.

Surrender to the Glow

Open eyes to the dawn's embrace,
Feel the warmth, a gentle trace,
In the silence, let it flow,
Surrender sweetly to the glow.

Life's a dance of joy and woe,
Find the magic in the slow,
Every heartbeat sings of grace,
In the light, we find our place.

The Hush of Lively Dreams

In the stillness, whispers weave,
Lively dreams that we believe,
Stars wink down from realms unknown,
Guiding paths where hopes are sown.

Midnight musings take their flight,
Painting worlds in moonlit night,
Every slumber holds a quest,
In this hush, we find our rest.

Whispers of Joy

In the quiet morning light,
A gentle breeze sings sweet,
Softly rustling through the trees,
It dances past my feet.

Laughter floats on carefree winds,
Carrying tales of old,
Each whisper a secret joy,
A treasure to behold.

In colors bright and bold,
Nature's palette paints the sky,
With every breath, I feel alive,
Embraced by joy, I fly.

Underneath the starry night,
Dreams twinkle, soft and clear,
In whispers wrapped around my heart,
Joy waits for me right here.

Hidden Radiance

In shadows deep, there lies a light,
A glow that softly gleams,
It dances in the quiet dusk,
Illuminating dreams.

A spark within the darkest night,
A warmth that knows no bounds,
It's found in every heart that beats,
In silence it resounds.

Through cracks and flaws, it shines so bright,
A treasure none can see,
Hidden radiance glimmers on,
Forever wild and free.

We walk the paths of radiant grace,
With every step, we find,
That beauty often hides from view,
Yet still, it is entwined.

Laughter Beneath the Surface

Beneath the waves, a world alive,
Where laughter hides and plays,
In bubbles that burst into delight,
It dances through the days.

Coral reefs hum gentle tunes,
As fish parade in schools,
Each flicker, each joyful cry,
In nature's playful rules.

Every wave that kisses sand,
Holds laughter soft and sweet,
In the rhythm of the tide,
Joy finds its steady beat.

With every splash, a story told,
A tapestry of glee,
Beneath the surface, life abounds,
In laughter's endless spree.

Glow of the Unseen

In twilight's hushed embrace I feel,
A glow that can't be caught,
It whispers in the fading light,
A truth I never sought.

Faint glimmers in forgotten paths,
Guide steps in quiet ways,
The unseen glow that leads me on,
Through nights and sunlit days.

In every breath, the warmth surrounds,
A luminescent weave,
We search for light in distant stars,
Yet here, it's ours to leave.

The beauty rests in what we know,
And what we cannot see,
For in the glow of the unseen,
Lies all that sets us free.

Inside the Glow

In the dark, a soft light gleams,
Whispers carried on moonbeams.
Shadows dance with gentle grace,
Hope ignites in this warm space.

Flickers of joy in the night,
Guiding hearts with pure delight.
Each glow a story waits to tell,
Secrets held within the spell.

Serene Chortles

Laughter bubbles like a spring,
Joyful echoes, sweet bird's wing.
Among the trees, the voices flow,
Nature's chorus, soft and low.

A melody bright, it twirls in air,
Filling hearts, easing care.
With every chortle, peace unfolds,
A tapestry of warmth retold.

A Surprising Grin

Caught in a moment, eyes align,
A spark ignites, a sweet design.
Unexpected turn, a shared gaze,
In a world lost, it sets ablaze.

From silence born, a grin appears,
Bridges built through shared cheers.
Like sunshine breaking through the gray,
In laughter found, we drift away.

The Warmth Beneath the Surface

Underneath the frost and snow,
A pulse of life begins to grow.
Beneath the cold, the earth does weave,
A tale of spring we can't perceive.

Whispers of blooms, yet to unfold,
A promise kept, a secret told.
With every thaw, the heart does beat,
Awakening hope in winter's seat.

Veil of Intimate Joys

In twilight's gentle glow, we find,
A whisper soft, a touch so kind.
The world outside fades away,
As hearts entwine in sweet ballet.

Beneath a sky of shimmering stars,
We dream of love, forget our scars.
The rhythm of our breath aligns,
In this sacred space, our souls combine.

Time stands still, an endless dance,
In every glance, a tender chance.
The laughter shared, the secrets told,
In this embrace, we feel so bold.

With every heartbeat, joy ignites,
In moments rich with soft delights.
Together here, we dare to soar,
In the veil of joys, forevermore.

Whispers of Joy

Softly spoken words we share,
In the quiet, love lays bare.
Glimpses of laughter fill the air,
A joy that's light, beyond compare.

With every smile, a promise bright,
A fleeting glance, pure delight.
In simple moments, bonds are tied,
In whispers sweet, joy cannot hide.

Dancing shadows under the moon,
Hearts in harmony, a sweet tune.
Together we weave a tapestry,
Of laughter, love, and harmony.

Each gentle touch, a spark ignites,
In the night, where dream takes flight.
Whispers linger, soft and true,
In the depths of joy, just me and you.

Radiance Unmasked

Behind the mask of everyday,
Lies a glow that lights the way.
Shadows fade, and dreams take flight,
In radiant hues, we claim the night.

With every laugh, the world we change,
In the dance of life, we rearrange.
Colors burst, like blooms in spring,
Unmasked joy, in freedom we sing.

A journey shared, hand in hand,
In unison, we take a stand.
Every heartbeat sings a song,
In radiance bright, we both belong.

With open hearts, we face each dawn,
In the light of love, we're never drawn.
Unmasked in truth, we rise anew,
In the brightness found, just me and you.

Echoes of Laughter

In the corners of the room, it fades,
A melody of joy, as time cascades.
Children's giggles, pure and bright,
In echoes of laughter, we find our light.

Memories linger in the air,
With every laugh, we show we care.
The warmth of love, a gentle tease,
In laughter's embrace, our hearts find ease.

Through ups and downs, we share the ride,
In bursts of joy, side by side.
Each echo tells a story sweet,
In shared laughter, our lives complete.

So let the laughter flow and swell,
In joyous sounds, our spirits dwell.
Through every chuckle, every cheer,
Echoes of laughter, forever near.

The Dazzling Depth

In waters deep where secrets glide,
Colors swirl and dreams reside.
Flickers of gold, a glimpse of night,
Echoes dance with soft moonlight.

Rippling tales on currents clear,
Whispers carried far and near.
Every wave a story spun,
In this realm, we're all as one.

Beneath the surface, life unfolds,
A tapestry of blue and gold.
In these depths, our spirits sing,
Cradled safe by the ocean's wing.

So let us dive, explore, and find,
The wondrous treasures intertwined.
In the dazzling depths, we shall play,
Forever lost, yet found, we stay.

Enchanted Absences

Beneath the trees where shadows weave,
A whisper flows, we hardly believe.
In twilight's hold, they softly sway,
The dreams that linger, then drift away.

Moonlight kisses the empty space,
Where echoes of laughter once found grace.
In absence, beauty takes its flight,
A haunting presence in the night.

Faded notes of a long-lost tune,
Sway with the leaves and sing to the moon.
In their silence, stories unfold,
Of cherished moments, brave and bold.

Yet in the heart, they find their home,
In every sigh, we are never alone.
For in enchanted absences, we see,
The beauty that was, forever will be.

A Silent Symphony

In the stillness, a melody flows,
A symphony of the heart that glows.
Notes unspoken, yet deeply heard,
In every sigh, a gentle word.

Each silence holds a hidden grace,
In quiet moments, feelings embrace.
The ripples dance on a tranquil lake,
A silent song, for memory's sake.

Gently drifting on dreams unchained,
Harmony where joy has reigned.
In the pause, the world takes breath,
A silent symphony, life and death.

Listen closely, and you will find,
The sweetest notes within the mind.
In the hush, let your spirit soar,
A silent symphony forevermore.

Whispered Jests

Under starlit skies, laughter plays,
Secrets shared in delightful ways.
With every jest, a bond does grow,
In silent smiles, we come to know.

Each wink and nudge, a playful tease,
Whispered tales dance upon the breeze.
In the corners where shadows meet,
Joyful echoes in rhythms sweet.

A glance exchanged beneath the moon,
Promises linger, hearts in tune.
In laughter's light, we shed our fears,
Whispered jests to dry our tears.

So let us revel in joy's embrace,
With every chuckle, find our place.
In whispered jests, life's simple art,
We weave together, heart to heart.

Secret Grins in Shadows

In corners where soft whispers play,
A smile lingers, shy but bright.
The moonlight dances, casting sway,
As shadows flirt with gentle light.

Eyes meet in the dim-lit glow,
A secret shared, a hidden jest.
In silence, hearts begin to flow,
As darkness wraps us, feeling blessed.

The night unveils its tender theme,
While laughter echoes 'neath the stars.
In whispered dreams, we dare to dream,
Our secret grins, our guiding scars.

So let us dwell in quiet thrills,
Where shadows hide our playful minds.
With every glance, a spark instills,
In this sweet realm, love gently binds.

Heart's Quiet Delight

In the stillness of the morn,
A gentle sigh escapes my lips.
The calm of day, a heart reborn,
As sunlight wraps its golden strips.

Each moment whispers soft and sweet,
In comforting embrace, I stay.
The rhythm of my pulse, a beat,
In nature's arms, I find my way.

A flutter of the leaves above,
A songbird chirps its lively tune.
These simple joys, a gift of love,
The heart's delight will always swoon.

Here in the quiet, peace takes flight,
In tranquil hours, my spirit soars.
With every breath, I feel the light,
A treasure found, forever yours.

Twinkles in the Depths

Beneath the waves, a world of dreams,
Where mystic lights begin to dance.
In shadows deep, the beauty gleams,
And silence holds a gentle chance.

Each flicker tells a tale of yore,
Of sailors lost and tides that shift.
In depths unknown, there lies a score,
A symphony of light's sweet gift.

Amongst the corals, secrets play,
The ocean's heart in rhythmic sway.
With every pulse and soft caress,
A love for all that thrives, no less.

So dive within, and you shall find,
A universe that twinkles bright.
In the depths, treasures intertwined,
A dance of dreams and pure delight.

Echoes of Inner Cheer

In quiet moments, truth takes flight,
A whisper of joy, a soft embrace.
The laughter lingers, pure and light,
In every heartbeat, there's a trace.

With every step, the joy will rise,
As shadows fade in morning's glow.
A spark ignites within our eyes,
In every echo, hope will flow.

The world spins on, but we stand still,
In harmony, our spirits sing.
With each heartbeat, warm and full,
The echoes dance on feathered wing.

So let us cherish every cheer,
In life's sweet melody, we find.
With open hearts, we draw near,
To echoes of joy, unconfined.

Secrets of Serenity

In whispers soft, the night unfolds,
A tranquil heart, in silence holds.
Beneath the stars, dreams take their flight,
In shadows deep, we find our light.

The gentle breeze, it tells a tale,
Of calmness found in nature's veil.
With every breath, let worries cease,
In stillness, we invite our peace.

Reflecting pools, like mirrors gleam,
Embrace the quiet, share the dream.
A world at rest, where thoughts can flow,
In secrets held, true wisdom grows.

Here in this space, our spirits mend,
With every moment, time will bend.
In harmony, the heart can steer,
Unlocking all, the secrets near.

Sweetness Unseen

A gentle hand, a soft embrace,
In fleeting glances, love finds grace.
The sweetness lingers, softly shared,
In hidden corners, hearts are bared.

With every laugh, a memory made,
In whispered words, our fears cascade.
The smallest joys, they intertwine,
In every moment, love will shine.

The hidden gifts, beneath the skin,
Like precious gems, they spark within.
In tender looks, we find our way,
Unseen sweetness, brightens the day.

With every step, a dance divine,
In every heartbeat, love will twine.
A world of warmth, though out of sight,
In currents deep, we find the light.

Bliss at the Core

In daylight's glow, there lies a spark,
A quiet peace, in every heart.
With open arms, we greet the morn,
In every sigh, new hopes are born.

Within the soul, a secret song,
In harmony, we all belong.
With every breath, a chance to see,
The bliss we seek is always free.

The gentle pulse of life unfolds,
In every moment, truth beholds.
In laughter shared, and dreams pursued,
We find the core of gratitude.

With eyes wide open, we explore,
The joy that ripples from the core.
In simple things, our spirits soar,
In every heartbeat, bliss does pour.

An Aura of Whimsy

With colors bright, the world ignites,
In every glance, a dance of lights.
Through playful winds, the laughter flies,
In wondrous dreams, imagination sighs.

The leaves that twirl in twinkling glee,
A land where hearts can dance and flee.
Beneath the willow, secrets speak,
In childhood's joy, it's joy we seek.

With every whimsy, let us roam,
In magic's glow, we find our home.
A tapestry of tales unfolds,
In dreams we weave, our truth beholds.

So take my hand, let's dance away,
In this delight, we'll choose to stay.
In every heartbeat, find our play,
An aura bright, come what may.

The Laughter Unraveled

In shadows deep, where whispers play,
Laughter hides, in a soft ballet.
Echoes dance on the edge of night,
Revealing truths that spark delight.

Through cracked masks, a gleam breaks free,
Joy spills forth like a wild spree.
Hidden smiles in the brightest glare,
Weaved in tales, lightly they fare.

Beneath the surface, ripples gleam,
A fleeting glimpse of a cherished dream.
With every chuckle, a secret shared,
In laughter's warmth, all hearts are bared.

So let them flow, these joyous tides,
In every jest, the spirit abides.
Unraveled joy, easy and bright,
We find ourselves in the soft light.

Mirth Beneath the Mask

Beneath the veil, a jest unfolds,
Crafted tales of the brave and bold.
With painted smiles, we play our part,
Yet deep within lies a tender heart.

In whispers soft, the truth will shine,
A flicker bright, like aged wine.
Through every riddle and every jest,
Mirth finds refuge, a welcome guest.

With laughter's echo, fears allay,
The masked dance leads us on our way.
In hidden joy, friendships bloom,
Creating light in the deepest gloom.

So let the masks be worn with grace,
For in their depths, there's a sacred space.
Mirth beneath, a bond so strong,
Together, we rise, where we belong.

Secret Springs of Joy

In quiet nooks where shadows grow,
Secret springs of joy do flow.
Nestled deep within the heart,
Where laughter waits to play its part.

A joyful leap through trials faced,
Moments cherished, never misplaced.
In sounds of nature, pure and sweet,
The beauty of life lends a gentle beat.

With every dawn, the light reveals,
The hidden grace that laughter steals.
In every smile, a treasure found,
In love's embrace, we're tightly bound.

So seek those springs, let spirits soar,
In every drop, the heart will pour.
Joy's secret springs, forever bright,
Leading us onward, pure delight.

The Brilliance Concealed

In silence soft, a fire glows,
A brilliance hidden, no one knows.
Like stars that twinkle from afar,
Glimmers of truth, our guiding star.

Beneath the layers, colors blend,
A vibrant heart that will not bend.
In whispered tales of jest and cheer,
Lies the essence we hold dear.

As clouds may hide the morning sun,
So too, our laughter is rarely spun.
Yet in each chuckle, we find our way,
A spark ignites, turning night to day.

So let it shine, that hidden light,
In every shadow, banish fright.
Brilliance concealed, yet ever true,
In laughter's warmth, we will renew.

Glimmers of Delight

A whisper of joy, so soft and light,
Dancing through shadows, taking flight.
In the heart of a moment, a spark ignites,
Filling the world with small delights.

The laughter of children, pure and free,
Echoes of love, like a sweet melody.
Each smile a treasure, a reason to stay,
In the glimmers of delight, we find our way.

Petals of blossoms, shades of the sun,
Each tiny heartbeat, a race just begun.
Touching the soul with a tender kiss,
In fleeting moments, we find our bliss.

Stars twinkle brightly in the night's embrace,
Warming the spirit, a gentle grace.
In the tapestry of life, we weave our part,
Glimmers of delight, a treasure of the heart.

Unseen Happiness

In the quiet corners, where joy resides,
Winds of contentment, a gentle tide.
A secret elation we often chase,
Unseen happiness fills every space.

The rustle of leaves, a breezy song,
Nature's orchestra, where we belong.
Each moment a chance to pause and sigh,
Finding serenity, letting time fly.

In simple gestures, a smile shared,
The warmth of connection, hearts laid bare.
Through laughter and love, we uncover the day,
Unseen happiness lighting our way.

A sunrise whispers, hope in its glow,
Reminding us gently, it's okay to grow.
In the tapestry of life, we find our bliss,
Unseen happiness, a world full of bliss.

The Quiet Radiance

In the still of the evening, a spark ignites,
Casting a glow, soft and bright.
The quiet radiance, a hush in the air,
Whispers of beauty, everywhere.

Moonlight filtering through the trees,
Creating shadows that dance with ease.
In serene moments, the heart takes flight,
Embraced by the peace of the velvet night.

Gentle reflections on a calm lake,
Ripples of dreams that softly wake.
In whispers of twilight, hope takes hold,
The quiet radiance forms stories untold.

Each sigh of the wind, a lover's tune,
Under the watchful eyes of the moon.
In the silent embrace, our spirits merge,
The quiet radiance, a sacred surge.

Veil of Cheer

Within the morning's tender light,
A veil of cheer takes gentle flight.
Carried on breezes, a joyful sound,
In every heart, hope is found.

With laughter echoing through the trees,
Swirling petals dance in the breeze.
Every moment births a chance anew,
A veil of cheer wraps around you.

In the glow of sunsets, colors blend,
Embracing the day, like an old friend.
Each whisper of joy, a chorus clear,
In the universe's embrace, a veil of cheer.

So let us gather, hand in hand,
Creating together, a joyful band.
With hearts united, forever near,
We wear the world's love, a cherished gear.

Radiance in Every Breath

In the morning light, we rise,
With hope that dances in our eyes.
Each breath a whisper, soft and clear,
A gift of life we hold so dear.

In the quiet moments, we find,
The warmth that warms the heart and mind.
With every heartbeat, dreams take flight,
A symphony of pure delight.

Through the trials, through the pain,
We seek the joy that will remain.
A spark of love, a touch of grace,
Radiance blooms in every space.

Inhale the beauty, exhale the fears,
Embrace the laughter, welcome the tears.
For in each breath, we come alive,
In this grand dance, we will thrive.

The Secret Dance of Delight

Beneath the moon's soft, silver glow,
A rhythm whispers, pure and slow.
The shadows twirl with gentle grace,
In the night, we find our place.

Laughter spirals, a sweet refrain,
As heartbeats echo through the lane.
The world fades, time stands still,
In this moment, we find our thrill.

Secrets shared with every glance,
In joy we lose ourselves, we dance.
The magic twines around our feet,
No greater joy than this heartbeat.

With every step upon the ground,
A tapestry of love is found.
In the dance of hearts, we unite,
In the secret, we find pure light.

Tucked Away Smiles

In corners hope and joy reside,
Tucked away where dreams can hide.
A gentle touch, a knowing glance,
In silence speaks the heart's romance.

Beneath the burdens of the day,
Lies a treasure hidden away.
With laughter stitched in every seam,
A quilt of love, a whispered dream.

The warmth of smiles we save for night,
Illuminates our darkest fright.
In fleeting moments, sparks ignite,
A heart that glows with soft delight.

So share a smile, let love unfold,
In the tiny things, we find the gold.
For in this world, while we roam,
Tucked away smiles lead us home.

Echoes of Inner Bliss

In stillness, hear the heart's soft song,
Echoes of a love, profound and strong.
Through windswept dreams and whispers kind,
We find the peace that we had mined.

Each thought a wave, each breath a shore,
Where echoes dance forevermore.
In moments woven with sweet grace,
Our souls entwined in endless space.

The laughter rings like chimes in air,
In solitude, we feel the care.
A gentle hum, a sacred tune,
Echoes beneath the silver moon.

The truth resounds within our core,
An endless journey, evermore.
In the symphony of life, we see,
The echoes of our inner glee.

Underneath the Mirth

In laughter's echo, shadows play,
Hearts bound together, night and day.
We dance on dreams, so light, so free,
Underneath the mirth, you and me.

Whispers of joy, in twilight's glow,
Moments of silence, where secrets flow.
The warmth of friendship, a gentle breeze,
Underneath the mirth, souls find ease.

With every chuckle, a ripple spreads,
Spinning tales where the heart treads.
Through storms we laugh, through trials we sing,
Underneath the mirth, love takes wing.

In shadows cast where joy is found,
We share our dreams, together unbound.
With every heartbeat, a promise made,
Underneath the mirth, we'll never fade.

The Joyful Veil

A tapestry woven with threads of gold,
Stories of laughter, timeless and bold.
Each moment captured, a gem in the sky,
The joyful veil that whispers why.

Beneath the layers, the colors blend,
Fragments of joy that never end.
Happiness dances, like light on the sea,
The joyful veil, just you and me.

With every heartbeat, a secret shared,
Echoes of gladness, our spirits bared.
Through trials deep, the shadows flee,
The joyful veil, our sanctuary.

In every sunrise, a promise bright,
Wrapped in warmth, in soft twilight.
Together we're stronger, hearts in sway,
The joyful veil, come what may.

Inner Sunshine

A spark ignites within my heart,
Chasing the shadows, tearing apart.
With every smile, the light will grow,
Inner sunshine, a radiant glow.

In quiet moments, I find my peace,
A gentle warmth that will never cease.
Through clouds of doubt, I choose to shine,
Inner sunshine, forever mine.

With laughter ringing, I spread my wings,
A melody of joy that softly sings.
Embracing life, with all its gifts,
Inner sunshine, the spirit lifts.

From every corner, light cascades,
Illuminating paths, love never fades.
In every heartbeat, let it flow,
Inner sunshine, we'll let it show.

Enigmas of Elation

In whispers soft, the secrets play,
Dancing with shadows, night and day.
Elation hides in laughter's grace,
Enigmas found in a warm embrace.

Through winding paths, adventures call,
Moments unspoken, we'll cherish all.
Each heartbeat sparks a mystery,
Enigmas of elation, wild and free.

In gentle breezes, stories unfold,
Joy wrapped in layers, precious as gold.
With every breath, let wishes rise,
Enigmas of elation in our eyes.

Together we wander, hand in hand,
Finding the magic in this land.
With joyful spirits, we ignite the flame,
Enigmas of elation, never the same.

Hidden Horizons of Hope

In shadows cast by doubt and fear,
Lie dreams that whisper, crystal clear.
The dawn will rise, a gentle tune,
To weave the light, to chase the moon.

With every step, the path unfolds,
Brave hearts will find the strength it holds.
Beyond the veils of darkened skies,
A tapestry of hope will rise.

So gaze upon the distant shore,
Where tides of faith will call for more.
In quiet moments, hear the sound,
Of promises that swirl around.

Through trials faced and battles fought,
The flame of hope cannot be bought.
With courage sewn in every seam,
We forge ahead, we hold the dream.

The Glow Within

In every heart, a flicker burns,
A whispered light, a gift that yearns.
Through darkest nights and stormy seas,
This inner glow will always please.

Like fireflies that dance in flight,
It guides us through the wildest night.
A beacon shining, soft and bright,
Illuminating paths of right.

Beneath the weight of heavy clouds,
A voice of joy, it speaks aloud.
In simplest acts, the glow is found,
In every laugh, in every sound.

So tend the flame, let it ignite,
A world transformed by love and light.
For in each soul, it yearns to shine,
A glow within, so pure, divine.

Joyful Echoes

In laughter shared, a bond so true,
Each note of joy, a song anew.
Like ripples on a tranquil lake,
These echoes make the heart awake.

With every smile, a spark released,
A gathering of joy increased.
In moments sweet, we dance and sway,
Embracing life in bright array.

Among the trees, the whispers grow,
In every breeze, their laughter flows.
From mountain tops to valleys wide,
These echoes ride the world's great tide.

So cherish each, let spirits soar,
For joyful echoes, we adore.
In unity, our hearts shall sing,
A symphony of everything.

Beneath the Laugh

Behind each laugh, a story hides,
Of hopes and dreams and secret tides.
A smile may mask the deepest pain,
Yet joy remains, a sweet refrain.

In playful jest, our souls align,
We share the warmth, the taste of wine.
Yet shadows linger, soft and shy,
Beneath the laugh, the truth can lie.

With every giggle, there's a thread,
A tapestry of words unsaid.
In every jest, a piece to mend,
A promise made, a heart to bend.

So let us laugh, and let us weep,
For life is both, the shallow and deep.
In every chuckle, find a way,
To bridge the gap, to heal the gray.

The Softest Beam

A whisper of light, so gentle and bright,
It dances through leaves, a sweet, soft delight.
In twilight's embrace, the shadows retreat,
As warmth from the sun makes the world feel complete

The sky starts to blush, with colors that play,
Brushing the canvas, as night fades away.
The softest beam shines, igniting the dawn,
With hopes that awaken, as darkness is drawn.

It kisses the earth, where the flowers bloom wide,
A promise of peace, in the morning's tide.
Nature's soft glow wraps the world in a hug,
The essence of life, a warm, cozy mug.

So let this beam linger, let it fill your heart,
In moments of stillness, where beauty won't part.
A reminder of grace that forever will gleam,
In the quietest moments, the softest beam.

Smiles in Silence

In corners of rooms, where whispers reside,
A bond made of laughter, but quiet inside.
Eyes twinkle softly, as stories unfold,
In the warmth of the night, their secrets are told.

A glance shared between, a comfort divine,
No need for a word, just a hand in mine.
Silence speaks volumes, in gestures so grand,
As smiles intertwine, like grains of warm sand.

In stillness, we find the moments that shine,
The heart's gentle rhythm, our lives interline.
Each pause is a blessing, a thread in the seam,
That stitches our souls in this delicate dream.

When words fade away, let our spirits align,
For in smiles of silence, our hearts intertwine.
Together we cherish the peace that we share,
In the beauty of being, we breathe the same air.

The Heart's Dance

Under moonlit skies, where shadows ignite,
The heart starts to twirl, a beautiful sight.
With every soft beat, a rhythm so true,
It knows all the steps, like a dance just for two.

The stars spin around, in a sparkling trance,
While melodies whisper, inviting the chance.
To jump and to sway, in this timeless embrace,
As laughter and love find their perfect place.

In moments of joy, when the world fades away,
The heart leads the way, in its intricate play.
With every soft step, it carves out the ground,
In the dance of the heart, our souls are unbound.

So let us sway gently, in the moon's silver light,
For the heart's dance is magic, a wondrous delight.
With each beat together, our spirits will soar,
In the rhythm of love, forever and more.

Layers of Light

Through prisms and hues, the world comes alive,
A spectrum of colors, where dreams start to thrive.
Layer upon layer, the sunshine will weave,
A tapestry glowing, in which we believe.

With each passing moment, new shades will unfold,
As stories of light in our hearts will be told.
The warmth of the sun, through branches it streams,
Painting the canvas of our waking dreams.

In whispers of dawn, where pink skies take flight,
The essence of hope is born out of night.
Layers are woven in the fabric of time,
In the glow of our lives, we find reason and rhyme.

So let us embrace this bright, endless show,
For in layers of light, our spirits will grow.
Together we shine, in this luminous flight,
As we dance through existence, in love's purest light.

Glittering Echoes

In the night where stars do gleam,
Whispers of past dreams do stream.
A soft light paints the silent dark,
Echoes of hope, a tender spark.

Beneath the moon's watchful gaze,
Life dances in a silver haze.
Footsteps trace a path of grace,
Chasing shadows, a timeless race.

With every flicker, secrets unfold,
Stories of hearts, both brave and bold.
In the silence, magic flows,
Life's symphony softly glows.

So let the night's embrace be tight,
In the stillness, find your light.
For in the dark, all dreams take flight,
Glittering echoes shine so bright.

Elation's Embrace

In the morning's golden rays,
Joy awakens, new day's praise.
With laughter sweet and voices clear,
Elation's whisper draws us near.

Clouds of doubt, they fade away,
As vibrant colors paint the day.
Hearts are light, horizons wide,
In happiness, we learn to glide.

A spark ignites in every soul,
Reaching out to make us whole.
Every moment, pure delight,
Wrapped in warmth, the future's bright.

So dance upon the world's grand stage,
Turn every leaf, unlock the cage.
For in this life, embrace the chase,
Let love and hope frame your space.

The Hidden Bliss

In the quiet, secrets bloom,
A garden thrives, dispelling gloom.
Soft whispers weave through tangled vines,
The heart's melody in soft signs.

Mountains high and valleys low,
In nature's arms, true treasures grow.
Finding joy in simple things,
The hidden bliss that kindness brings.

Raindrops dance upon the leaves,
Each pulse a promise that believes.
A gentle touch from earth to sky,
In unity, we learn to fly.

So seek the magic, slow your pace,
In every moment, find your grace.
For in the stillness, joy will flow,
The hidden bliss, let it show.

Radiant Roots

Deep in the earth, where life begins,
Are radiant roots, where strength spins.
They weave a web of timeless grace,
Embracing all, in every space.

From ancient tales, a legacy,
Nurtured soil, in harmony.
Branches reach for the sky above,
In every leaf, a tale of love.

Seasons change, yet still they stand,
Facing storms with a steady hand.
In every trial, roots dig deep,
Guarding dreams as we gently sleep.

So honor the ground that holds you tight,
For in your roots, there's endless light.
With every heartbeat, grow and thrive,
Radiant roots keep dreams alive.

Joys Wrapped in Silence

In whispers soft, the shadows play,
A melody that draws the day.
Gentle thoughts like petals fall,
In stillness found, I hear their call.

Beneath the weight of quiet skies,
The heart finds peace, where silence lies.
In every breath, a treasure found,
In tranquil moments, joy abounds.

The world outside may rush and race,
But in this calm, I find my grace.
Wrapped in stillness, dreams take flight,
From shadows bloom the purest light.

So let us hold this sacred space,
Where silence reigns, and we embrace.
For in these joys, both small and grand,
Life's sweetest truths, in silence stand.

Hidden Gleam of Happiness

Beneath the clouds, a spark ignites,
In secret glades, the heart takes flight.
A flicker bright in muted hue,
Transforms the gray to vibrant blue.

In laughter shared and smiles exchanged,
The hidden glimmer feels unchained.
A secret laugh within the soul,
A dance of joy that makes us whole.

In quiet corners, treasures gleam,
Reflections of a cherished dream.
A soft embrace, a gentle sigh,
In harmony, our spirits fly.

The small delights, they weave a thread,
In every moment, joy is fed.
So seek the gleam in every day,
For happiness is here to stay.

Serene Laughter Within

In the chambers of the heart, it stirs,
A laughter light that softly purrs.
Amidst the chaos of the day,
It whispers softly, come and play.

With every giggle, fears release,
In playful moments, find your peace.
The warmth of joy, like sunlight shines,
A balm for life's entangled lines.

In deeper stillness, laughter glows,
A gentle tide that ebbs and flows.
It dances forth in pure delight,
While shadows fade to welcome light.

So let it rise, this laughter sweet,
In every challenge, feel its heat.
For in our core, it dwells within,
A treasure trove where joy begins.

Gleeful Murmurs Lurking

In hidden nooks, a soft voice calls,
Echoes linger, joy enthralls.
With every rustle, stories weave,
A tapestry that we believe.

Gleeful murmurs, secrets shared,
In shared moments, none compared.
Through laughter's lens, we start to see,
The beauty held in harmony.

The breeze brings forth the sweetest tune,
In twilight's glow, beneath the moon.
Whispers dance upon the air,
A gentle touch, a bond we share.

So listen close, the joy is near,
In every murmur, love is clear.
For in the quiet, hearts align,
In gleeful whispers, souls entwine.

Inner Shimmer

In shadows deep, a light will gleam,
A flicker bright, a waking dream.
It dances soft, it glows so clear,
Within the heart, it draws us near.

A gentle spark, it warms the night,
A hidden truth, a guiding light.
Embrace the glow, let worries cease,
In inner peace, we find our ease.

Through trials faced, it starts to grow,
A beacon bright, in winds that blow.
Unfolding strength, it leads the way,
Our inner shimmer, come what may.

And as we tread this life's grand show,
We carry forth that radiant glow.
Illuminate the path ahead,
With every step, let love be spread.

Whispered Gleams of Hope

In twilight's hush, a whisper calls,
A glimmer soft, as daylight falls.
Through shadows cast, a promise gleams,
In hearts awake, igniting dreams.

The winds may chill, the storms may roar,
Yet hope persists, it seeks the shore.
In every tear, a seed is sown,
A whispered gleam, we're not alone.

With every dawn, new light will break,
A chance to rise, new paths to take.
In silence made, the courage grows,
From whispered dreams, our spirit glows.

So let us weave, our tales untold,
With whispered gleams, in hearts of gold.
Together strong, we'll chase the light,
In whispered hope, we find our flight.

Heartbeats of Happiness

In laughter's sway, our spirits soar,
With every beat, we crave for more.
A moment caught, in time we cling,
Where joy resides, our hearts will sing.

Like ripples cast on tranquil seas,
Happiness flows, a gentle breeze.
In shared delight, we find our place,
Each heartbeat echoes, love's embrace.

Through sunlit days and starry nights,
In every glance, our joy ignites.
Together shine, as fears recede,
In heartbeats shared, we plant the seed.

Let's dance through life, with open hands,
In every step, our laughter stands.
With heartbeats racing, dreams in view,
In happiness found, I'll be with you.

Subtle Joys

In morning light, a flower's bloom,
Unfolding grace, dispelling gloom.
A fleeting touch, a soft embrace,
In subtle joys, we find our place.

The rustle leaves, a whispered song,
In nature's arms, where we belong.
A gentle smile, a knowing glance,
In simple moments, we find our dance.

The warmth of sun, the taste of rain,
In tiny wonders, we break the chain.
From mundane tasks, our joy deploys,
In life's rich fabric, we seek the joys.

So let us cherish, the little things,
For in their sway, our spirit sings.
In subtle hues, our world enjoys,
A tapestry woven, of subtle joys.

Joyful Shadows

In twilight's glow, the shadows dance,
Whispers of joy in a fleeting glance.
Children laugh as the day bids farewell,
In playful tones, their secrets swell.

The trees sway gently, cradled by breeze,
Time stands still beneath the tall leaves.
With every twirl, a story unfolds,
In joy's embrace, our hearts are bold.

Stars begin to peek from the sky,
Lighting the canvas where dreams can fly.
Together we roam through night's gentle hue,
In joyful shadows, just me and you.

The moon casts silver upon our skin,
With every moment, new adventures begin.
Let's chase the whispers of tomorrow's call,
For in joyful shadows, we can have it all.

Laughter's Embrace

In the soft glow of morning's light,
Laughter bubbles, pure delight.
Echoes ring in the sunlit air,
Joyful moments we freely share.

Children's giggles fill the park,
Playing freely until it's dark.
Every game a world of dreams,
Laughter dances in vibrant beams.

Around the table, stories soar,
Voices mingle, that's what we're for.
In the warmth of friendship's grace,
We find comfort in laughter's embrace.

Let the smiles be our guiding light,
Together we'll shine, taking flight.
In every heartbeat, a spark ignites,
In laughter's arms, life feels just right.

The Light That Lingers

At dusk when daylight starts to fade,
A soft glow whispers, unafraid.
Golden rays touch the earth anew,
Painting the world in vibrant hue.

In corners where shadows used to play,
The light weaves magic at the end of day.
Every edge kissed by a gentle beam,
Revealing beauty as if in a dream.

Moments cherished in fleeting time,
Memories linger, rich and sublime.
The heart holds close what the eyes can't see,
In the light that lingers, we are free.

So let us chase that fading sun,
With every heartbeat, our lives as one.
In twilight's glow, we touch the divine,
In the light that lingers, forever we shine.

Beneath the Exterior

Beneath the surface, stories lie,
Hidden treasures waiting to fly.
With careful hands, we peel away,
Layers of life where shadows play.

In the smiles that cover the pain,
Resilience blooms like gentle rain.
Every scar holds a tale untold,
In the heart's garden, love is bold.

Through the cracks, hope seeps in slow,
Blooming where the wild things grow.
In every whisper, a truth appears,
Beneath the exterior, we face our fears.

Let us embrace what lies inside,
For vulnerability, we don't need to hide.
In unity, let our souls collide,
Beneath the exterior, love is our guide.

Hidden Gleam

In shadows deep, a light can hide,
A quiet spark, where dreams abide.
Beneath the veil of dark and gloom,
A whisper waits, to break the room.

A glimmer soft, like stars at night,
It dances shy, just out of sight.
Yet in its warmth, the heart ignites,
The hidden gleam, our true delights.

With every turn, we seek its face,
In secret places, find our grace.
For even in the darkest scene,
There lies a glow, forever keen.

So trust the path where shadows blend,
For every journey has an end.
And in that light, we shall remain,
In hidden gleam, we break the chain.

Sunlight Beneath the Surface

Rippling waters, deep and clear,
Hold the warmth of sun so dear.
Beneath the waves, a radiant glow,
Quietly waits to let us know.

In whispered tides, the secrets dwell,
Stories told by the ocean's swell.
Sunlight dances in a soft embrace,
A hidden world, a sacred space.

When shadows fall and doubts arise,
Look for the light, be wise and wise.
For in the depths, the truth will rise,
Sunlight shines bright, a sweet surprise.

With every breath, we find our way,
Through murky depths where hopes can fray.
A flicker calls from dark's periphery,
Sunlight beams forth, setting us free.

The Secret Grin

In crowded rooms, I catch your eye,
A fleeting glance, a silent sigh.
Your secret grin, a hidden spark,
Igniting joy, igniting dark.

A playful tease, it dances near,
It speaks of dreams we hold so dear.
In laughter shared, our souls entwine,
The secret grin, both yours and mine.

Through whispered thoughts and gentle sighs,
We find a world that never lies.
In every moment, soft and thin,
There blooms the joy of that secret grin.

So let us wander hand in hand,
Through realms uncharted, dreams unplanned.
For in this warmth, our hearts begin,
To thrive and leap with that secret grin.

Heart's Hidden Glow

Beneath the noise, a stillness beats,
A quiet pulse where longing greets.
The heart's hidden glow, a tender flame,
Aspect of love, none can tame.

In secret corners, we shall find,
The whispered hopes of heart and mind.
Where shadows linger, light will flow,
Transform the dark with heart's glow.

When doubts arise and shadows creep,
Hold close the dreams, a promise to keep.
For in the depths, they brightly show,
The boundless love, the heart's hidden glow.

With every breath, we rise and sing,
Awakening the gifts we bring.
In unity, we brave the storm,
With heart's hidden glow, forever warm.

Resilient Radiance

In shadows deep, where hope may wane,
A flicker glows, igniting flame.
Through storms we stand, with courage bright,
Our hearts endure, embracing light.

Each trial faced, a lesson learned,
With every bridge, our passions burned.
Resilient souls, we rise anew,
In waves of change, we form our crew.

The stars align, our paths intersect,
With every step, our souls connect.
We shine through tears, we laugh through pain,
In radiant hues, our joy remains.

Together strong, in unity's grace,
We dance through life, we find our place.
In every heartbeat, a vibrant song,
Resilient radiance, we all belong.

Uncharted Happiness

In secret nooks, where laughter blooms,
We chase the light, dispel the glooms.
With open hearts, we wander wide,
Through uncharted paths, joy is our guide.

The sun peeks through the leafy trees,
Whispers of joy carried by the breeze.
With every step, the world unfolds,
In simple moments, true wealth beholds.

We paint our dreams in colors bright,
With brushes dipped in pure delight.
Each smile shared, a spark ignites,
In uncharted realms, we find our heights.

A treasure map of sunny days,
In laughter's echo, our spirits blaze.
Together we shall roam the land,
Uncharted happiness, hand in hand.

Illuminated Pockets

In pockets deep where secrets hide,
We find the glow, our hearts abide.
With whispered dreams, we share the light,
Illuminated truths, shining bright.

The warmth of friendship, tender, near,
A silent language, crystal clear.
With flickering hopes, we weave our fate,
In these small pockets, love runs straight.

The stars have tucked their light away,
Yet still we find it in the day.
With gentle hands, we lift the shade,
In illuminated spaces, memories made.

Each little joy, a beam we hold,
In every heart, a story told.
Together bright, we paint the night,
In illuminated pockets, pure delight.

Subtle Glee

In morning's light, a gentle sigh,
Moments fleeting, as clouds drift by.
With quiet smiles, we find our way,
In subtle glee, we greet the day.

The rustle of leaves, a soft refrain,
Echoes of joy, like gentle rain.
With every glance, the world aligns,
In whispered laughter, contentment shines.

We savor tea on sunlit porches,
A symphony sung by nature's torches.
With tiny blessings, our hearts expand,
In subtle glee, together we stand.

Each fleeting moment, a precious gift,
In soft embraces, our spirits lift.
Through simple pleasures, we come to see,
Life's sweetest treasure lies in subtle glee.

Reflections of Bliss

A quiet stream flows soft and clear,
Mirroring skies that shed no tear.
Joy dances lightly on the breeze,
Whispering secrets among the trees.

Golden rays in morning's spread,
Chasing away the dreams we've fled.
Gentle moments, time stands still,
In every heart, a tender thrill.

Petals fall like whispers sweet,
Embracing ground beneath our feet.
In every glance, a story shared,
In silence, love is gently bared.

Together we find our sacred space,
In each heartbeat, a soft embrace.
Reflections linger, bright and true,
In every moment, me and you.

The Cheer That Lingers

A laugh like sunlight in the morn,
Brightening souls, a joy reborn.
Every chuckle, a thread of light,
Binding us close, a shared delight.

Fleeting times we hold so dear,
Echoing warmth, drawing us near.
Gathered moments, memories weave,
In every smile, we dare believe.

Whispers of fun in the evening air,
Painting our skies, with colors fair.
Every jest, a spark ignites,
Filling our hearts on starry nights.

So let the cheer forever stay,
In shadows or sun, come what may.
For in the laughter, love takes flight,
A radiant glow in darkest night.

Brightness Beneath

Beneath the clouds, a sun still glows,
In hidden places, warmth bestows.
A gentle hum of life persists,
In quiet corners, joy exists.

Each raindrop carries tales untold,
Of vibrant dreams and hearts so bold.
In nature's cradle, peace unfolds,
A treasure trove of memories gold.

Among shadows, colors bloom,
Awakening hope, dispelling gloom.
Through every crack, the light shall seep,
Whispering promises to keep.

So pause awhile, and look around,
In every heartbeat, light is found.
In subtle ways, life's joys are sewn,
A tapestry of love we've grown.

Harmony in Hushed Laughter

In quiet rooms where whispers play,
Laughter dances, soft and gay.
A gentle touch of joy unfurls,
Embracing both our hearts and whirls.

Faint echoes linger in the night,
As smiles blend with the soft moonlight.
In jest and jive, our spirits soar,
Creating bonds that we adore.

The world outside may thrash and roar,
Yet in these moments, we explore.
Every giggle, a precious tune,
Resonating with the stars and moon.

Together we weave a spell so rare,
In laughter's arms, we shed our care.
So let us cherish this sweet song,
In harmony, where we belong.